The Spy Who Bluffed Me

ANDY RIVERS

10 Dec 2022

is a good friend of mine.
i gave this book to a book seller
on the streets of colombo.
i want to see how far it can travel.
Please tag him on instagram
    @ byker_rivs
oh... and get checked!

Published by:-

Byker Books
Bridlington
East Riding of Yorkshire
YO15 3PX

www.bykerbooks.co.uk

Typeset by Byker Books, Bridlington

ISBN: 9798352460924

ABOUT THE AUTHOR

Andy Rivers has been a Butlins barman, pretend chippie on a Spanish construction site, coach holiday rep, mobile sandwich salesman and outdoor traffic cone washer to name but a few of his eclectic 'career' choices. Originally from the East End of Newcastle he now lives on the Yorkshire coast where, as well as defeating Bowel Cancer in a 'straightener' in 2022 and following Newcastle United around the country, he passes the time by indulging in his passion for 'Professional Geordieism' and beer. This is his fourth published tome (he is also the author of **'I'm Rivelino'** – a hilarious account of the forty years of hurt he has suffered at the hands of the Magpies, **'Maxwell's Silver Hammer'** – a uniquely written, gangster thriller set in Newcastle and **'Special'** a loosely connected follow up also set in Newcastle.)

With the royalties from these books he plans on buying an Aston Martin, drinking copious amounts of Gin Martini and having a proper mid-life crisis.

He may be waiting some time.

CONTENTS

For Lisa. For MacMillan, for Stoma Nurses, for the NHS
and for everyone, everywhere who's battling Cancer.
Keep ya chin up and keep fighting.

To everyone else…GET CHECKED!

Rivs

PROLOGUE

ONE CLEVER FUCKER

You won't know it from looking at me right now but I am one clever fucker.

Granted, I'm covered in blood, tied to a chair and stark bollock naked but that doesn't detract from my cleverness, no way kidda. And, if that wasn't enough, as well as being clever I'm also The World's premier close protection operative.

Well, I say The World's...probably more like England's...well I say England's, strictly speaking I'm probably more like the North East's...well I say the North East's...oh fuck off gobshite I'm good and that's all you need to know.

You're thinking now aren't you, *if he's that good at protection and if he's that clever then how come he's still tied to that chair, covered in claret and has all his white bits on show?* You probably think the room I'm in's not that cosy either. Bare walls, one little light bulb with no shade – tramps eh? No windows, no carpet and one door. Looks locked, you can tell that kind of thing when you've been in and out as many houses as I have in the course of your career history.

I'd have to give you that like, I know how it looks but you have to remember that not only am I a clever fucker and hard as nails with it, I'm also bloody lucky so I'll probably get out of this.

How did it come about then I hear you ask?

Same old story innit, thinking with the little head instead of the big one. Well, that and the businessman's curse, tried to diversify too soon see.

As I've said, top close protection operative me. Good name in the business, making a fortune an' all. Made fifty notes last week helping out a local celeb with a little problem. No names no pack drill, gotta have discreets in this game matey. Just know this, if you was to watch the local news one night and one of them presenters seems to have a bit of a cold – well it aint Lemsip they're snorting that's all I got to say on the subject like.

Anyways, despite me being a clever fucker, I got side-tracked by a bird didn't I. There I was minding me own business getting bucket loads of respect off all the main faces through me superior protection business. Got regular numbers on quiet little doors an' all. Well… one door. Actually, it aint that quiet either, mind you, keeps me sharp that does. You needs to stay on your toes and that when you're putting your name up to do the door at The Shattered Beaver keeps your name in the frame and your game at the top of the division.

Or something.

Like I says clever fucker me. You think I'm thick don't you. That's why my bollocks is dangling through this chair and my nipples have got them clamps on. Just like my teachers at school, won't give no-one a chance you fuckers. They all ganged up on me an' all and then put me in the dippy sets cos I was too much for them. Thirst for knowledge see, always asking questions, no good to them when they want a quiet life is it?

Anyways, my kind of clever ain't that book shit that geppy fucking students do is it? No way, you want my kind of clever you've got to be street smart. Think Rocky mixed with Spender, add in some Terry McCann and season lightly with a bit of Del Boy. Stick in an oven made by Ray Winstone and then give it two hours in Al Pacino style heat – oh aye, that's fucking me to a T that is. So, me teachers, well cos I ain't their kind of clever, I ends up in the nut huts with the dipshits and the squawking fuckers, couldn't hear myself think half the time. Lucky I was handy with me fists or I'd have been in trouble with them weird twats. That's how I got the nickname, you've probably heard of me, Neville 'Pagga' Palmer?

No?

Fuck it your loss. Anyways, you're obviously interested in me story or you wouldn't have bought this book would you? You'd better have fucking bought it an' all mind. If you've swiped it then the bloke in the shop won't get paid and if he don't get paid then neither do I. If I don't get paid then you'd better be ready for a big, pissed off Geordie to come through your front door at two o clock in the morning wearing his favourite knuckle duster you thieving bastard.

Well, just as soon as I gets meself loose from this predicament anyways.

So, this bird, she offers me the chance to do a bit for King and Country and that. I knew there was something dodgy about it but she was paying cash in hand so me giro was safe and even though she had cracking jugs it wasn't them what swung the deal, oh no, I'm a professional me remember.

She's connected ain't she? You know, secret service, on his Majesty's and all that palaver. She's a fucking spook and that. So, I'm thinking, do this job right and there might be some lucrative work at the end of it, get me off the door at the Beaver for good like.

Well, that and I might get to shag her.

So, anyways, she's the reason I'm here and the reason I'm going to get me gonads flayed with knotted rope in a bit – yeah I've seen that James Bond film, I know what's coming. Might be the last thing coming for a while like, depending on what state me nads is left in.

Tell you what, seeing as we're here I might as well tell you the whole fucking thing while I can still talk with a man's voice an' all

CHAPTER 1

KICKING IN THE BACK DOORS

'Progress Report 001. '

'Sir. Target confirmed as loose lips. Has fatally compromised 009 with enemy and aborted operation 'Industrialist'.

'As we suspected. You know what to do 001.'

'In hand Sir.'

'Good. They take out one of ours, we take out one of theirs. Carry on.'

'Very Good Sir. Over and out.'

So we've gone back a little while right. It's a couple of weeks ago, might be three, not sure really, hard to tell when your napper's as busted as mine is at the minute.

Fucking cold in here with no strides on an' all. Just as well my spook bird ain't here, I'd have nothing to impress her with at the present moment in time if you know what I mean. Well, obviously she'd be impressed by my cleverness and my sparkling repartee and that but physically? Well as I say it's cold and I'm naked so fuck off you cheeky twat. I tell you this an' all gobshite, you can mock but you wouldn't like it between the cheeks of your arse....or maybe you would you fucking weirdo.

Anyways where was I, oh aye, it was Friday night and I was doing my regular door at the Shattered Beaver. It was all going smooth as the silk on a posh girls pyjamas when they turned up. Cosgrove and Bobbin.

They're professional rivals see, them two. We all treat each other with respect, you have to in this game, but it's obvious they're checking out the competition and, as I say, I am the number one protection operative around these parts.

'Alright Spacca.'

That was just their little joke. It was a respect thing.

'Lads.'

We always went on like this, we was all mates together in this game and the camaraderie, even between rival firms, was a big part of the job. Bobbin gave me a humourous slap round the back of the head and we all had a laugh. He's crap at slapping like, I could feel his knuckles on me napper so he'd obviously bunched his fist. Fucking amateur.

Cosgrove stood square on to me and put his head into mine, it was like there'd been an eclipse. I couldn't see nothing but scar tissue, indian ink and false tan. Reminded me of a bird I'd nailed the week before, same aftershave as well come to think of it.

Anyways, he growls something about me not stopping them coming in and we has a laugh about that an' all. Professional courtesy ain't it, you always lets the competition see how well you're doing an' that. So I stood aside told them to get a drink by all means. We're all mates ain't we and they smiled back. Well Cosgrove did, Bobbin did the closest thing he could to a smile and then gave me another jokey slap in the solar plexus before they went in.

'Great lads them two,' I said to the waiting queue at the door when I got back up.

They was all looking at me and smiling so they knew we was just messing about,– all lads together like. Anyways I quickly dropped the first fucker at the front with a short right just to be sure, too good looking to drink in here anyway that one, when the manager comes out to see me.

'I don't want the likes of Cosgrove and Bobbin in here Pagga. I pay you to keep them types out of here so do your job….and why's that twat on the floor with a broken nose?'

I had to think quick, luckily I'm a clever fucker.

'You know how you wanted me to find out who'd been sniffing round your daughter boss…'

Not strictly a lie as the smarmy fucker had been in here last week trying it on with her but a bit of a fib 'cos the boss wanted to actually know who had been shagging her but being his daughter he didn't want to use the actual word. And matey on the floor hadn't been up to none of that with her, I knew that for a fact. That's cos it was me what was actually doing her and what with her studying for her A levels and the gymnastics class she was doing as well as the secret pole dancing lessons I knew she didn't have time for no-one else.

He bought it anyway, kicked the bloke in the nuts and told him he was barred.

'Right well done, now get them two fuckers out my bar.'

Now I had to be thinking carefully about this. Cosgrove and Bobbin were obviously no problem to a man of my physical proportions and fighting knowledge. Oh no, when it comes down to the old personal protection game then they were strictly second division or whatever it's called this week. I mean I may have mentioned this before but I am the head honcho round here and a clever fucker at that. No these boys would present no problem to me in a physical sense but I obviously had the reputation of the pub to think about. When the gaffer had first took over the boozer and took me on he'd said he wanted to give the place a better rep. You know make it a good night out for couples and that. I remember it clearly 'cos I'm a professional in this game me.

'Pagga, If any bird's trying to get in here and she's got more tattoos showing than skin then knock her out. Any bloke what drinks halves is out an' all, we're not a pink palace are we?'

So, you know, management directive weren't it? I know he didn't actually say 'don't go scuffling with them two big scary bastards Cosgrove and Bobbin and getting your body smashed to bits,' but I'm sure that's what he meant. It's all about customer service this job, know what I mean, interpret the punters needs and give them what they want.

It's what I told his daughter anyways.

Thinking back my first night there was a good 'un an' all. We'd just shut the place for a lock in with the regulars, they was all appreciative of how I'd busted heads all night like, and the curtains was closed then there's a noise at the back door. Old Jackie peeps out the window then ducks back again white as a sheet.

'There's two lads trying to get in with a crowbar.'

Then there's a crash and the fuckers swing open, the two thick bastards didn't realise we was all there did they? They were dealt with quickstyle like.
If I could have got there before old Jackie I'd have done them myself but he twatted them with his zimmer and they fucked off. Shame about his bag bursting and that, meant he couldn't drink the pint the gaffer give him, still I made sure it weren't wasted and we all gave him a little wave as they put him in the ambulance.

As I was saying to the landlord's daughter later on - imagine having your back doors kicked in like that.

Anyways though, you're thinking again now ain't ya. You're thinking well how did good old Pagga get them lunatics…I mean protection professionals like myself…out that bar without it all kicking off and him having to use his extensive defence techniques and training. Have I mentioned I'm a fighting expert as well as a clever fucker? No? Ah well it'll probably come up in conversation sooner or later.

Well, like I say, I knows me way round a bag of spanners me and I know how to skin a cat. Not that I ever have like. Shaved a few pussies kidda but not skinned no cats, oh no not me and the RSPCA will never prove nothing neither. So, Cosgrove and Bobbin, get them out without having to use me world famous one-two combination. Easy.

'So that's sorted lads aye. Same time next week?'

'Aye Spacca, nice doing business with you – you fucking pleb.'

Jokers them boys, they really are. Bobbin gave me a witty little backhand in the gob by way of saying goodbye and that was it sorted. Now dafties like you wouldn't understand, you just see a scared bouncer giving two local head the balls money to fuck off and leave him alone but you'd be wrong wouldn't you.

What you really saw was a business transaction between professional men who know that spilt blood is bad for reputations and cashflow. I gets paid fifty a night for being on that door and I gave them twenty bar each. That means I'm still in profit and there's no bother – well no more than the usual but I can handle a couple of stabbings and the odd riot.

Told you I was fucking clever.

Anyways that's how it happened. Normal night, normal stuff happening.

Broke up a couple of fights in the bogs, took the drugs off some cheeky bastards who'd brought their own in and got a quick BJ off Capri, the landlords daughter, before she went to her evening class.

So, nowt out the ordinary, until I seen her. I was hanging about the back door of the boozer watching this bloke what had been knocked over by a white van and laughing at the pissed up twat trying to get up when this vision of beauty jumped out the back of the van. Blonde she were, like the head of a pint of Guinness. Curvy in all the right places an' all, think of ooh…a knuckle duster. Sexy as fuck mate, the way she booted him in the head and then axe kicked his ribs fuck me I had such a hard on. When she pulled out her gun and slotted the cunt without a seconds' hesitation I knew I was in love.

I've never been in love before, well pies don't count do they, and I wasn't exactly sure that's what it was but I reckons this must have been it. Is it love when your arse clenches like you're trying to stop a fart escaping? Or when your heart tries to come out your mouth and punch you in the face shouting "it's love you fat get now do something," I don't know but it must be something like that eh? I wasn't sure what to say, me mouth had dried up and me hands was shaking so I took the pint and joint off a passing underaged hoodie and quickly necked the both of them.

Then, it happened. Our eyes met across the road and there was this instant magnetism. Actually it might have been a proper magnet I dunno, but she was across that fucking road and on me in a flash. She had an earpiece on and I could hear a tinny voice shouting at her through it. He was saying something like *Usual decoy out of commission. Send replacement.*

Thinking about it now maybe the fucker shouting had the same treatment with the rope and the bollocks as I'm going to get – fucking voice sounded awful man. Anyways, she grabbed me lapels and looked me straight in the eyes, I knew I was a good looking twat but this was ridiculous. I could feel her gun in me bollocks, well I hope it was her fucking gun I didn't want none of that shite I got into in Thailand again – fucking nightmare that.

Then she spoke.

'What did you just see?'

Her voice was like cut glass. I reckoned she'd grown up riding ponies and playing lacrosse...whatever the fuck that is. Mind if she'd had that sort of power between her legs on a regular basis it was no wonder she was jumping old Pagga, know what I'm saying? I think you do.

'I just saw you pet and then there was nothing else in the world worth looking at.'

Heard that on an old film, I always used it. Worked every fucking time. Nothing surer.

'Problem averted. He's a dick. No threat. Repeat no threat.'

I knew she'd done that to keep me safe. It was obvious she was protecting me 'cos I had something she wanted. Oh aye, definitely had something she wanted. And then she was gone. Back in the van with the tin man. One last look and she was off. I knew that wouldn't be the end of it though. She had that glint in her eye, I know women I do and I knew she'd be back for more of the Pagga experience.

I was right an' all.

Clever fucker me.

CHAPTER 2

LITTLE RED RIDING HOODY

'Progress Report on Plan B 001.'

'Prospective Trojan Horse selected. Approach imminent Sir.'

'Very Good. Quick work 001. Do you think he's up to the task?'

'Seems pliable enough Sir. And big and tough. Should be enough for our needs.'

'Excellent. I'll leave it with you.'

'Thank you Sir. Over and out.'

The next day I've still got her on me mind haven't I? Keep seeing her everywhere, it's like I'm hallucinating or something. Honest, I mean to look at me you'd think I'd never done anything unhealthy in me life – body of a Greek god and all that – but it's like all that acid I did in the eighties has come back to haunt us. I'm at Texan Pete's having my normal morning fry up, trims the fat off the bacon mind – I'm not a fat bastard me, when I see her face behind a newspaper on the bench across the road. By the time I'd put the seventh sugar in me tea and looked back up she was gone, must have imagined it.

I eats me brekkie, taking the opportunity to nick a couple of sausages some ungrateful bastard has left on their plate next to my table, honestly there's some fucking wankers in the world. Mind you they was cold by the time Pete had turned his back long enough for me to neck them, still waste not want not eh? I wish I'd give the fried egg a miss though, the bloke was livid when he come back from the bog. So anyways, I does me morning vittles and then I'm at the bookies checking out the form and casually counting up the change in my pocket, never let the bastards in there know how much you've got, you'll never leave the place alive, when I clocks a movement in the window opposite and it's only her checking out my form. Well that's what I thought like, I puts my fifty pence treble on and looked again and there was no-one there, have to give my head a shake I think.

Maybe this is the love thing again?

I thought on it for a bit and then decided that even though I'm a clever fucker there's just some things in life a bloke don't know about and this love shite's one of 'em. I always thought love was invented by blokes, to keep birds happy and to sell 'em books or something. Like a marketing ploy that's just gone too far 'cos everyone believes in it now. Fuckin hell – maybe that's how Jesus started? It'll be that Diana next – nowt surer.

Anyways you don't want to hear old Pagga philosophising, you aint as clever as me for a start, you wants to hear the story. So with this love shite in mind and how it was affecting my sight, funny like cos I thought it made you go blind not see things but there you go. Like I says, with this in mind I decided to approach an expert on the subject so I heads to the Baited Badger, old Maureen the landlady knows the game. She should anyway, she was on it fucking long enough.

'Pagga, what you after son, usual?'

'No Maureen, I'll just have a drink cheers.'

I waits til' she's poured the beer before I ask my question, if you give her too much to think about at once she goes to pieces. No she literally goes to pieces, bits of her skin fall off through stress and I didn't want her bits in my mouth, not again.

'What do you know about love Maureen?'

'It's an expensive game Pagga, an expensive game son.'

She lets go a big rasping, tar addled cough that nearly dislodges the fag from her lips and a fucking awful smell fills the air. Too late I realise she's used the cough to disguise one of her legendary farts and I know I need to get the beer to my mouth to filter out whatever's been up her arse this week. I tell you what though, she's fucking over-rating herself if she thinks her love's expensive, last I heard she cost somewhere in the region of twenty five pence and a pickled egg. Still, should hear her out anyways.

'Aye, you need to make sure the lass loves you and when you know that for sure you never let her go kid. Anything else and you're set for fall, a hard one an' all. That's my advice.'

I'm still gulping my pint and using it as an air filter so I try to just nod but it's hard 'cos I can't breathe and the beer's gone up my nose instead of down me throat. Fucking hell. I start coughing and she's round the bar patting me on the back.

'You alright son, you need a hand?'

'I ain't got no cash Maureen.'

'Oh fuck that then,' she takes her wrinkled old digits off me bollocks and gets back behind the bar.

'Why you asking anyway Pagga?'

'Well I spotted this bird and we had an instant connection like and I can't stops thinking about her. I keep seeing her everywhere an' all. It's like she's following me, I tell you Mo me napper's not right with it all'

She cackles away, flashing them pearly yellers at me then bends forward over the bar giving me the overhead view of what looks like a pair of labradors ears. Fucking old labrador an all, still got pink noses like.

'You got it bad son if you're seeing her everywhere. Hey, don't suppose you can see her instead of me can you?'

'Told you Maureen I'm skint.'

'Fuck it, a girl's gotta try Pagga.'

I drains the pint and head off, she gives me a wave and goes back to filling in her claim form for that accident she had with the stairlift, don't know how she got it up there in the first place meself mind. No time for pondering that though cos what's she's said has puggled me head. She reckons it must be love and she would know, I mean she's a bird for a start and she's seen more cocks than a vasectomy doctor. Fuck it, had to happen sometime. I just needs to sort out the other bit now then, make sure she's in love with me like so I don't fall over, that'd be embarrassing.

17

I'm thinking about things so much I doesn't notice the little gang of hoodies what's got round me as I turned the corner into the back of the shops, about ten of the little fuckers. They all know me like. Big Pagga they calls me, I'm like a hero to most of these boys. They's been hearing tales about me from their mothers' for years. In fact I recognise one of them, young Duane, I reckons I've done his sister you know.

'Alright lads?'

The biggest one moves forward, proper trying to make a claim for leader of the gang by not smiling and by waving a blade about. I decide to humour him and help him out by pretending to be worried.

'Ya talking diss stylee to me blad cos I is a girl innit ya cheeky meff.'

What? Why does no cunt talk proper anymore? I can see where this is heading and I can't be arsed so I shoves the nearest one out the way and moves off. Fucking kids you try to help them and they takes liberties. Next thing I know they've all jumped me and I'm on the floor. Must have slipped. They's all on me though and I can't move. Young Duane's got his face in front of mine and he's holding a blade near me neck now. You know thinking of it I didn't do his sister, it was his mam. Must 'ave been about ooh, fourteen year ago. I smiles to myself, he'll have heard some tales about old Pagga I'm betting.

I can feel some hands on me pockets and my blood rises. The cheeky little fuckers, I start thrashing about to gets them off when the knife is pushed against me throat. Bastards.

'Luk 'im pissed 'imself. Yah yah yah.'

Take no notice of that, it's a trick I learnt at fighting school when I was training to be Britains premier protection operative. They'll get off me now so's they don't get piss on them. Then I'll kill them.

I can feel the weight moving off me legs, told you the piss trick would work, and there's a bit of screaming but I can't see what's going on 'cos young Duane's just staring at me close up. Like he's looking in a mirror or something. Weirdo. Then he's yanked off and thrown against a wall. There's another hoody on the scene and he's beating fuck out of all 'em.

'You're lucky he's doing that you little bastards 'cos once I get up I'm going to kill all of ya.'

And I will kill them all when I get up. You've got to get up slowly though when you've been down like that.. That cramp can be murder on the legs you know. By the time I'm up and swinging they're all either spark out or fucked off and my little helper's covered in teenage claret – we've all done that though eh? He looks over, probably to say thanks to me for letting him help me out. It must be that love thing again though. My new mate's the spitting image of my spook bird, fucks sake my heads a mess man, he/she gives me a wink and next thing I know I'm on me jack again. There's a siren in the distance and I decide to vacate the area, fucked if I'm getting the blame for this so I heads back to the bookies. Not that I gets the chance to get in the door like, two of the fuckers come rushing out with their walking sticks, waving them like swords or summat.

'What are you two at you daft old bastards?' I greet them.

'Fuck off Pagga you fat, over-rated cunt.' One of them jokes back with me.

'Get out of the way fatboy, there's a crew of hoodies hanging round and we're going to do the little shits.'

'No need boys,' I say, 'Pagga Palmer's done the lot already, check the claret and bodies up the road if you don't believe me.'

They nip up for a quick shufty and comes back all impressed.

'Fucking hell you only did it,' says the one with the least amount of wrinkles.

'I thought you was fuck all,' says the one with the badly made falsies, 'just a big fat bag of wind and piss.'

I can feel me hackles rising at this, I knows I didn't actually do them little scrotes but I would've once I'd gotten up proper, still don't hurt to take the glory now and then do it. Clever fucker me see, have I mentioned that?

'Let's get a cup of coffee in the bookies Pagga, on us for your heroics like.'

So we did and you know what, my nags had only come in and all. Proper good day that was and it only got better 'cos guess who turned up when I was drinking my winnings at the Badger later on. Got it in one –you're not such a fuckwit after all are you? – and even better, it really was her this time, not just my imagination.

CHAPTER 3

TRAINING DAY

'Progress Report 001.'

'First contact made with Trojan sir. Background checks ongoing and leverage points identified. Extremely confident of a positive outcome'

'Good Job. Remember, keep focused on the big picture and finish the job.'

'Yes Sir. Over and out.'

So obviously I've picked up me winnings and headed straight back to the Badger haven't I? I mean it's true what they say about money burning a hole in your pocket ain't it? You can look all blank and shake your head but I knows kidda, I knows. I had this mate right, let's call him Dave, well that's what his mother did and who are we to argue eh? He wins a load of cash at the bookies. Manages to get it home without mishap – which was lucky 'cos every fucker knew he'd won it and was planning on tapping his napper once or twice to get some beer tokens – and is in the living room just feeling it in his jeans. Well you know how it goes. That much money is exciting ain't it? It's early Saturday evening and Baywatch is on, he's a single man so he ain't betraying nobody and the inevitable happens.

The fire brigade reckoned it was friction that caused the spark that set the cash on fire in his back pocket. You know how the scouts rub two poles together? Well he only had the one to rub but he still managed it, he should have got a badge for it really. After he got out of hospital and we was all taking the piss out of him in the pub he looked a bit sad so I cheers him up.

'Hey Dave,' I says, 'you knows how you always wanted a black cock – well wish no more my son.'

He didn't look too happy about it but the rest of the boozer was in uproar – no fucking pleasing some people. Miserable stumpy dicked twat. Anyways, as I said, it's bad luck to keep that much cash in your poke without spending some to relieve the danger. I was now the proud owner of twenty two pound and seventy eight pence and I was gonna spend the lot. Obviously as a professional protection operative I knew me limits and I remembered I was at work later on.

'Pint of lager and a whisky chaser Mo.'

'Got a few quid then Pagga have you?'

'I just wants drinks today Mo – needs to keep my strength up for working tonight.'

'Can't blame a girl for trying though Pagga, you can't blame girl for trying.'

So I'm sloshing them down and listening to the accounts of my bravery echoing round the bar.

'I heard old Pagga there gave a few of 'em a slap and told them to get out of the area like.'

Old? I ought to fucking give him a slap.

'Well I heard he beat shit out of all of 'em and told 'em he'd kill 'em all if they came back.'

Oooh good one.

'Nah, the truth is he beat shit out of 'em 'cos they was about to mug a pensioner and then when they didn't say sorry he killed the two biggest with his bare hands to teach them a lesson. Won't be seeing them little fuckers around here no more.'

Quality, any advance on that?

'Yous are all wrong. I heard he beat shit out of'em, dragged 'em all home and killed all their parents for having the cheek to bring devil spawn like that into the world. God's honest truth and may he strike me down if I'm telling porkies.'

You might be in trouble there son if the big lad's listening – nice one though. Gives the Pagga legend a bit of a boost.

'I know what happened…'

Shit it's Billy the Liar, this'll just be fuckin' stupidly over the top and make me look a cunt.

'He was getting a hiding off them little kids when a bird in a hoodie came along and saved his big fat arse. That's what's happened, I know 'cos I was watching them all from my window.'

The bastard. They're all looking at me then at him. I pull a *'are you gonna believe Billy the Liar?'* face and they look undecided. Then, just as I'm looking to see if the fire exit's still padlocked, one of them clouts Billy in the head and throws him out.

'Fuck off Billy that's just ridiculous.'

I hears the door go and turn around to tell Billy to fuck off again but the hairs on the back of my neck prick up as I swivel round and I reckon I know before I even see who it is. Yup, it's her.

My first thought is one of relief that she's changed out of that red hoodie. My second thought is that this must be fate if she's only wandered into a bar that I'm in purely by chance and my third thought is fuck, I hope she don't think I'm buying her a drink. The whole bar's looking at her but she don't give a monkeys, spook training see, they teach you not to show any fear or nothing. I know 'cos I've done a bit myself.

Don't look at me like that smartarse 'cos I aint fucking joking. As the number one protection operative in the immediate vicinity I've done all sorts of training I have. Weight training, Football training, Manual handling training oh yeah all the certificates me. My spook training though that was a bit special, not everybody does that. You have to know where to look to pick that sort of stuff up. Listen, I like you, even though you're a cheeky twat you seem alright, so I'll tell you how to go about it in case you fancy being a spook an' all. I mean you won't be in my league will you but not many are you know what I'm saying. Anyways, you go into town and you look for a place with a little 'D' sign on the front, that's the first part of your training see – awareness. If the 'D' is followed by these special spy symbols and hey, they've gotta be in this order or they don't count, so that's another spook thing, remembering symbols. What was I saying, oh yeah, they gotta be in this order after the 'D' right, like this '*e b e n h a m s*'.

Well when you see that you walk straight in without looking back, 'cos they're watching you know, and you looks for the special spook area. It's usually hidden in the '*Gift*' section. Whadya mean why?

Right, I'm a clever fucker and you're not so I'll try to put this easy for ya. You know how you can hide something by blatantly putting it in front of everyone? No?

Well you know how them politicians hide the fact they're all lying, cheating, whoring, corrupt and immoral bastards by going on the telly and denying everything even when their pants are still round their ankles and the office junior's still attached to their cock? Yeah, with me now? Good you've got it. Well it's exactly like that. Even though it's staring you in the face, because it's so blatant you can get away with it.

So you go to the middle of the shop, find the '*Gift*' section and find a stand full of pictures of cars and parachutes and stuff. Again, the name on it's a bluff that all us trained ops know about. I mean '*Big Day Out*', who'd fall for that shite? Jesus, not everyone's in this country's thick, present company excepted, no offence like.

What you do then is you poke about the picture things, they're like plastic cases, until you find one with the secret code on it. Now the code isn't that difficult to crack but then I am a clever fucker so maybe it is I'll let you decide.

'*Spydays – fun for all the family ages 7 and up.*'

See how they hide it – brilliant.

Anyways, there'll be a picture of a bloke in a dinner suit on the front looking all suave and that- that's so people who isn't in the know gets the wrong idea and think it's to do with restaurants or summit. What you do then is you takes the case thing up to the counter and hand it to the bird, she takes your cash without a word, proper spook she is you can tell by the way she chews her gum and ignores you while you pays your hundred and fifty quid. If she was normal she'd be flustered that you knew but 'cos she's had the training she can hide her nerves see, just carries on talking to her mate about shagging some gluesniffer called Darren while she's pocketing your cash.

So you've got the goods, now you just have to get home and ring the number and arrange your training. I did it mate and it's fucking brilliant. Screeching cars, unarmed combat, learning to talk proper and best of all you can take as many of the high tech gadgets what they've got as you want. Well no-one said I could take them but I did so fuck 'em. I was surprised at the amount of kids there but they've gotta train 'em young haven't they? It was good for 'em an' all when I was pushing in the queues and that for cars and taking their turns as well – character building and that. You can't be a spook and protect this country without a bit of the right stuff in you and I knows I've got the stuff in me all right. Specially after me training and sorting out them kids dads. It was funny how the spymasters on the course said not to come back, I reckons they was making me a sleeper, ready to be called upon when the country needed me.

And that time's now 'cos she's walking straight towards me. I'm gulping and fingering one of the gadgets in me pocket – The eavesdropper they called it, fits in your lug and lets you listen to people talking from half a mile away. I got some other stuff at home an' all but this is my favourite – I don't use it much like on account of what I hear people saying about me sometimes but it's still my favourite. Honest you wouldn't believe how good it is, I was using it once and I heard these two proper slappers talking in town about Ant an' Dec and a gimp mask, they was saying…oh hold on, no time for that she's here.

'Hello Mr. Palmer.'

I could feel myself twitching as her ice blue eyes looked me up and down, well one part of me was twitching anyways, big part an' all, well it was then but it was warm in the Badger, know what I'm saying?

'Hello again pet, how can I be of assistance.'

You've got to go through the motions and let them think you're polite and nice until after you've nailed 'em, they can find out about the real you after that – little tip for you there son.

She looks straight at me, I think she does anyways, I don't really know for sure 'cos I'm staring straight at her chest, magic man. Then I hears that voice cutting right through my defences again, it's definitely love this like.

'Your country's in trouble Mr. Palmer and we need your help.'

CHAPTER 4

BEACH HEAD

'Progress Report 001.'

'Trojan acquired, signed, briefed with as much detail as he requires and completely on board. My default approach worked well on this occasion.'

'Excellent. So Operation Industrialist' is go.'

'Yes Sir. Further updates as and when. Over and out.'

So what's a man to do?

I knows what you would have done son don't I? You'd have been straight in and fucked up your chances wouldn't you? But me kidda, no way. I know women and I know how they work.

'What's in it for me then?'

She leaned right in to whisper in me ear and as she did the back of her hand brushed me leg. Fucking second zip I'd broke that month.

'Your country would be very grateful, but more importantly...so would I.' She didn't so much say it as breathe it through my ear and into my head. It echoed round me brain for a bit and then headed south. Yup the zip was proper fucked now.

'Look Pagger's got a cherry on.'

'Fuck off Mo.'

'And a hard on.'

'Fuck off Mo – I still ain't paying for a handjob.'

'Can't blame a girl for trying Pagga.'

My posh bird beckoned me outside and that's when I found out how I could be of assistance alright. I mean I'm following her right, thinking she's taking me to shag alley out the back and trying to remember where I left me blobs from last time, I'm hoping I don't have to re-use the one from yesterday – you can only turn 'em inside out so many times can't you? When she takes a sharp left and we're next to that fucking white van again.

'I'm not getting in there love.'

'You don't have to worry about anything Neville – I would never hurt you.'

I'm trying not to look at her cos if I do I'll lose all self control and be in the back of that van quicker than Kerry Katona can get on the front pages of a shit magazine with another *'exclusive'* about *'getting my life back on track'*. Instead I concentrates on the graffiti on the walls leading down shag alley, some new stuff on there. Looks like Mo's dropped her prices, 'bout time really, she had fuck all else left to drop.

Some cheeky cunt's wrote something about me an all.

PAGGA PALMER SUX COX IN LIFTS FOR TEN PENCE BY COSGROVE

PAGGA IS A HOM AND SOFT AS SHITE BY BOBBIN

If I find out who's done that I'll kick their fucking heads in.

I was standing there raging and forgot all about my posh spook for a minute but she was soon back breathing in my ear.

'I need to show you something and I need your help Nev. Please jump in the van and we can brief you – you'll get paid.'

I turns to look at her, bright red lipstick shining in the chilly sunlight, my gaze goes downhill fast and it's obvious there's a nip in the air.

'Right you are pet – but call me Pagga.'

'Okay Nev…Pagga, in you go.'

The back doors swing open and an arm comes out to help me in. I gulped, only cos I needed some fresh air like, no other reason, no reason at all, then I stepped in. I wasn't scared. When you've faced down the hardest characters in the hardest town in the hardest country in the world then a little thing like getting into a van full of spooks that you saw kill a bloke in cold blood only the night before is nothing.

No I wasn't scared, I'd just had a bad pint that was all.

'Jeezuz, he's facking shat himself'

'Nah mate, just farted like'

'Scraffy Norvern cant...'

Lucky for that geppy twat he's an officer of the King or I'd have fucking lamped the soft cockney ponce, I still might actually if he keeps his noise up. Glasses or not.

Once I got into the van I realised there was nowt to be scared of, not that I was anyway like, it's the same as one of them you see on The Bill and that. All screens and wires and buttons that just have to be pressed.

'What's this one do?'

'Don't touch that you cant – you'll set the smoke spreader off ...ohhh fackin hell..'

'Cough...cough...what's that one do?'

'For facks sake, Vic tell your goon to keep his hands to his facking self – no sir no need to scramble the jets, false alarm sir. Sorry sir.'

My spook bird took my hand and sat me down at the side of the van, she looked deep into my eyes and, while I knew she was bang into me, for the first time in our relationship I was troubled.

'Vic? You didn't used to be a bloke did you?'

She just laughed, well I think she did I was watching her tits jiggle.

'It's short for Victoria Geordie boy,' then she leans in, all husky like in my ear again, 'I promise you, I'm all woman.'

'Right then so where we off pet – back to yours for coffee and that eh?'

See, I know when to make my move, she'd thought there was a chance of losing me and now I was making my move. Some blokes think they're players but me – I invented the fucking game man.

'No we're going to drop you off at yours and on the way I'll put the proposal to you and you can decide whether you're in but first you'll have to sign this.'

'What is it?'

'The official secrets act – if you tell anyone what I'm about to tell you then I'll have to kill you.'

She's a joker that girl. Kill me before she gets the chance to shag me – no chance man. I'll sign it anyway just to humour her but I know women me and she's gagging for it. Probably just not allowed to do me till I've signed up to be a spook – aye that'll be it. Probably have to prove meself on this job before she can get permission off her superiors to give in to her natural urges and get a piece of the Pagga action. Aye they don't let them shag civvies do they? Best get on with it then.

'Right then pet, what do I need to do, how much will I get paid and when do I get the spook gadgets?

She just laughed, crossed her legs again, flashing very nice thighs that I hadn't noticed before, and shook her head.

'All in good time my big hard northern friend, all in good time.'

I crossed my legs.

'Sorry I didn't realise you could tell.'

I fucking love the way she says big and hard, I'm gonna buy pants with no zips I think if I'm going to be working with her for much longer.

'What I want you to do is meet me tomorrow night at the big shady looking warehouse on the cliff top at the coast. The one with the strange lights that are on all night with the really fierce looking security guards. Do you know the one?

I knew the one she meant 'cos when we were younger me and some of the lads went to rob it. Don't look at me like that, we all have to make a living and Mo was younger then an' all so she could charge more. Anyways, four of us went in and twenty seconds later only three of us came out with a pack of rottweilers nipping at our arses. Never did find out what happened to little Tommy Trampsvest – it was his idea an' all. We said nixy to the law when they came round looking for him – well no point in all of us getting nicked an' all was there? If he'd moved quicker he'd have been alright and I wouldn't have teeth marks in the arse of me strides. Selfish bastard really, just a fucking excuse that false leg was, 'more life in a tramps vest' we used to say of the lazy twat. Still, he's gone now and because of him I know where the warehouse is and will probably get a top shag out of it so I should thank him really.

And I will. Once he's apologised for that fucking Rottweiler biting my arse.

'Aye. Shall I wait in reception then?'

I quite fancied that. Coffee from an office bird with sexy glasses and a tight blouse. Her having to kiss my arse 'cos I'm a spook an' that. Not that I needs that kind of power to make sexy office birds kiss my arse anyway. That thing what happened at the DSS was a totally different matter.

I'm snapped out of it when I twig she's laughing at me.

'You don't knock on the target's door and tell him you're there silly do you?'

See. Distracted. Birds always distract me. Made me forget me training an everything. God's to blame really for making me too desirable for them, just another cross to bear for old Pagga and, as that pretend Jock with the freaky blonde hair once croaked, I bears it well.

She must have noticed my dismayed face and thought I was backing out 'cos she looked all sad and then looked at the geppy cunt then back at me.

'He said you wouldn't be able to do it. Can't you try Pagga – just for me pleeeasee.'

Well firstly I was raging cos that cockney nob had no-classed me, then I was melting cos she looked so sad and then I was just as horny as fuck when I saw them lips pushed together to say please.

'Aye okay then but I'll have to give me notice at the pub tonight – did you mention summat about cash earlier?'

'We'll put five thousand pounds into your bank account at the end of the operation. Oh and Nev...I mean Pagga, if you can't see me around there then make your own way in. You can do that can't you? Clever, tough, big boy like you? Remember though, quiet and invisible.'

Then she leans forward giving us a good top view down her blouse.

'And there might be a little bonus in it for you at the end...'

Right then, where's the bus stop? I'm heading down the coast.

CHAPTER 5

OUT OF THE DOOR

'Progress Report 001.'
'Minor hitch sir. The Trojan has personal issues with a couple of likely lads in the same industry as him.'
'Is the problem surmountable within the time-frame?'
'I believe so sir.'
'Good. I'll leave that up to your discretion.'
'Very good Sir. Over and out.'

So I've got a lot to think about right?

The Country needs me. I've got to chuck me job in on the door of the Beaver, leave all of me other responsibilities – them Viagras don't sell theirselves you know – and travel to the back of beyond all in service of the King.

Now I'm a patriotic man I am, when duty calls I don't falter me. I'm in them trenches with the rest of the boys propping the flag up, eating mud and taking potshots at the enemy I am. So there was no need to ask me twice. Well, especially not when there was a grand a week and the prospect of getting jiggy with Vic the spook in the mixer and remember that's short for Victoria – she's not a bloke like, I don't care what you say.

So I rocked up to the Beaver to start me shift with pride in me heart that I'd finally been activated by the powers that be but there was a tinge of sadness an all. I mean I'd worked hard to get this door, this was the hardest pub in the area and being the head man here meant something. I was at the peak of my chosen profession and giving it up would be hard. Standing here at the weekends meant I beaten all them teachers who told me I'd be nothing. It meant I'd won against the cunts that used to beat me up and nick me dinner money and it meant I had respect. Mind you, even more important than that like – it meant I got birds, loads of 'em.

Case in point being the landlords daughter. She looked like butter wouldn't melt in her mouth, in fairness like it probably wouldn't cos there was never much room in there to fit anything else when I was around. Know what I'm saying kidda? But, she was the type of lass who wouldn't look twice at Neville Bloggs on the street. When Neville turned into Pagga though and started knocking charvas out left, right and centre then she couldn't get enough and that's what being on the door gave me. Respect...and like I said fanny.

So, as I dragged me carcass towards the classily pebble dashed exterior and the Oak style doors the memories came flooding back. Like that time I battered Pieman Pete, my nemesis from school, cos he'd grabbed the barmaids tits. I remember it like it was yesterday.

'Get your hands off her tits Pete – the doctor said they wouldn't set for another week you'll leave dents you cunt.'

'Don't speak to me like that Pagga, you were fuck all at school and you're fuck all now. You might be full of steroids and yeast these days son but I still remember the skinny twat who wore free school uniform and had patches on the knees of his trousers.'

The bar was full, I hadn't been there long and Pieman had a bit of a rep. Mainly cos of his nickname. He'd went into Greggs pissed up with a shotgun and demanded pastries with menaces – stupid twat got three years and now he was out he was trying to be top dog again. He had to learn things had changed and I knew it was my chance to assert myself and move towards my goal of being the top protection operative in the World. That was what my shrink said I had to do like after that 'episode' I had. Set myself targets and work towards them, move away from the past. I fingered the little surprise I had for him in my pocket and looked at the Pieman – goals and targets, aye that was good cos all I could see was a fucking big target.

'Hey Pieman, use your loaf son.'

He fucking hated the nickname and he hated me, only fair I did shag his sister at school…and his mother after…and his…no leave it there – she's in a home now.

Anyways he was coming my way and it was time to make my move.

'She's only trying to earn a crust man.'

The 'surprise' was now round my fingers and my right hand was up and in position – wouldn't be the first time neither but no time for jokes now mind. He came at me grunting like a bear having a shit, his big red face matching his big round body. He was raging. That made him careless, told you I was a clever fucker.

'Don't take the piss out of me you raggy arsed twat.'

I dodged to one side as he telegraphed the right hand he wanted to bury in me face and slapped his fat bald head. 'Now, now Pieman. Let's not mince about – are you chicken or are you just Steak and Kidding around?'

He went mental and tried to pick a chair up so while he was bent over with his back to me I clouted him in the back of the head. The steel knuckle duster did it's work and he hit the ground hard – the punters all gasped and word spread round town quicker than Jodie Marsh spreads her…butter on her toast. If little Neville had of been present with his national health glasses, patched up uniform and his free school meals voucher he would have approved, actually he'd have glassed the fucker while he was on the floor, Pagga had arrived and life wouldn't be the same again.

Now I was giving it all up, even though it was a good career move it was still a sad day like.

'Pagga where the fuck you been you fat cunt?'

Fucking shit job this – I can't wait to leave.

'I've had a bit of business boss – got something to tell you.'

'Fuck your business. I pay you to start at eight o clock not half fucking nine. I had to cover you with young Trev the glass collector. He looked fucking ridiculous in the bow tie – you know he's got a spotty neck.'

'Yeah but…'

'I also pay you to keep the shite out but what's happened?'

'I divvent kn…'

'I'll tell you what. Before you graced us with your presence a load of twocers turned up and kicked off with the squad of football lads that were in. Fuckin glass everywhere, claret up the walls and Trev's acne lefts it's mark on the carpet alright. Fucking pus soaked right through to the cellar.'

'I'm here now, I'll sort…'

'No fucking need now is there they've all gone. Luckily two proper doormen turned up. Cosgrove and Bobbin dealt with them all, changed my opinion of them lads now I have. In fact Pagga, fuck it, you're out. I need someone reliable for this job not a drunken has been.'

The cheeky bastard. Sacking us before I get the chance to quit. After all the hidings I've given out for him.

'Hold on boss. I've done the job fine for you in the past. Sorted out people that no-one else would. Remember Stinky Barry? No fucker else would throw him out would they? Wouldn't even touch him would they cos of the shit on his clobber? He just did what he wanted in every bar in town but I dealt with him didn't I?'

'Aye Pagga, Barry was a feather in your cap but that was then, this is now. You're yesterdays man. Cosgrove and Bobbin they're the future.'

Right you prick. Time to play this clever.

'Fair enough, where's me wages then?'

'Here, I've paid you for the weekend even though you've only done the one night. I'm a fair man Pagga and I hope you'll respect me for it.'

I took the money off him, give it a quick speed count just to be sure and then, when I was happy he hadn't diddled me, I dropped the nut straight on the fucker.

'Yesterdays man you cheeky prick – how did that feel then?'

'You'be broke by dose you Bat Funt…'

'I'll tell you what else I broke you fucker – ask your daughter what happened to her fucking cherry…'

Shite – that was stupid. He'd have put the popped hooter down to experience but nailing his pride and joy – fuck it, I've got the cash and I'm out of here tomorrow.

'BAAASSSTTTTTAAAARDDDDD.
COSGROVE, BOBBIN, GET OUT HERE..'

'Right must be off, got an early start at me new job the morra. Nice working for you boss – see you around eh.'

And that was me. Finishing one chapter as the number one Personal Protection Operative in the world and starting another as a top Spook with world safety as my responsibility. Look out James Bond cos Pagga's coming – wouldn't be the first time neither.

CHAPTER 6

BOBBIN AND PEEVING

'Progress Report 001.'
'Trojan appears to have resolved personal issue with hostiles of his own accord - impressively so.'
'Any input needed from your end?'
'No sir. I may need authorisation to try something further down the line though if required.'
'Consider it given. '
'Over and out.'

So I headed straight down the road to the Baited Badger. It's what you do innit when you've got time off work, you go straight to the boozer. It's even better when it's not expected an all and I've even been paid for it – fucking top banana that. The night's just getting dark and the lights are twinkling inside the boozer – it's all a bit Christmassy like. Funny how you can see in there now that people can't smoke in pubs anymore, never even knew they had fuckin windows before that. Nah, tell a lie, I chucked someone threw them once. Still a shock though – the place looks busy. I have to stop and think about it, I haven't been in here on a Saturday night for yonks, always working before wasn't I. Looks like it's proper buzzing can't wait to get into it and have a right good night – give meself a proper send off and that.

I slam the door open, all full of meself and ready to tell everyone how I told him at the Beaver to shove his job up his arse. Just bursting to proclaim my independence and how I've took meself off of the hamster wheel.

'Alright Pagga, heard you got the push up the road.'

Fuck sakes talk about bursting your bubble.

'Nah telt him to shove it like – got something else lined up.'

'Not what I heard. Story is you were told to fuck off by Trevor the glass collector and he give you a slap when you wouldn't vacate the premises.'

Billy the liar, can't bothered with his shite so I just give him a look and he gets the message – mind you booting him in the plums while I distracted him with me look probably helped.

'That's right crawl off you one bollocked freak.'

'Has Billy only got one bollock?'

'He has now.'

I've got a pint set up and I'm surrounded at the bar by the regulars, couple of birds listening to me tale as well at the edge of the group so I'm obviously embellishing a wee bit – hey, all's fair in love and shagging eh?

'So that was it really. I nutted the gaffer, ransacked the till, made mad passionate love to his daughter and left her in tears when I told her I couldn't marry her cos I was a love

and leave 'em kind of lad and then I sorted out Cosgrove and Bobbin when they shoved their noses in.'
Everyone's oohing and aahing at that like. A couple of the birds licked their lips suggestively when I said 'made love to' I might use that phrase again didn't realise it meant shagging till the other day when I was watching a chick flick on the telly – fucking melts them by all accounts.

'You sorted out Cosgrove and Bobbin? How did you do that then?'

Fucking Billy again.

'I telt them to fuck right off or to sort it out there and then – they took the first option'

Them lasses are grinding against each other now, oh aye they love a bit of violence women.

'If that's the case…'

'Billy man, I'm fucking busy here…'

'I'm just saying, if that's what really happened…'

Right he's getting another boot in the plums that twat – Can he not see I've got trailer trash hanging off me every word and soon to be hanging off me nadgers.

'Billy do you want another foot in the knackers? What is your problem?'

'Well I'm just wondering why, if Cosgrove and Bobbin are so scared of you, they're looking in the windows of this very boozer with 'Where's Pagga cos we're going to kick his fucking head in' expressions on their faces?'

Shite.
'What you doing down there Pagga?'

'Lost a contact lense'

'You don't wear them'

'Aye I didn't mean mine. I was in here with a lass the other night and she lost one, I was just looking for it like.'

'Right – nowt to do with Cosgrove and Bobbin looking for you then?'

'Nah, telt you man, I sorted them two already. Yesterdays men they are kidda. Are they still there?'

'Nah, they fucked off down the road, probably checking out 'The Painters Inn' and 'The Hand Shandy' looking for you.

That's me off the floor and flexing the guns.

'Lucky for them pair of cunts like. I don't want to be introducing them to the boys here – you don't buy these fuckers at B & Q, know what I'm saying'

I've still got the crowd round me lapping it up so I kiss the old biceps. Won't be the only thing getting kissed an all the way that Marie Capri Ghia and her mate Chantelle Mercedes Benz are giving me the once over – I reckon I know their mams as well..

'Glad you feel that way like Pagga cos I was just in the Beaver and heard the landlord offering them a grand each to do you in – something to do with his daughter…'

Have you ever thought how sick you would be if you ate a plate full of salt mixed it with shit and topped it off with double cream. You'd be puking everywhere wouldn't you, proper nauseous and that. I was anyway the time I did it, anyways, imagine just how sick you'd be and then double it.

Then double that.

Then double that again.

That's how sick I felt about then.

'The fucker's turned white, you alright Pagga?'

'You don't look well son, what's up?'

'Bad pint I think like'

That's all I could get out. My mind had stopped working. Cosgrove and Bobbin were coming for me.

'He's fucking scared isn't he…big soft shite.'

Fucking Billy again – he's always had it in for me that old twat. Even when I was a kid he'd get the other lads to bully us – tosser. Me mam used to go out with him apparently and then kicked him into touch when she had me, mustn't have got over it the bitter twisted old get. Well fuck them all cos I'm working for the King now. I bids me goodnights and heads off – early night I think. Just need to get home and get some kip. Me guts were still heaving a bit as I headed back to the flat. Cos it wasn't hoying out time yet there was no fucker about so the streets were quiet. That meant all I could hear was me heart beating every time a shadow danced across a streetlight. Not through fear like, just surprise and adrenalin and that. That's why I was a fucking nervous wreck as I rounded the corner to my stairs, not fear – adrenalin. Anyways there was a figure loitering at the bottom of the stairs so I had to do a double take, only fucking Bobbin wasn't it.

And where he was Cosgrove was never far away.

I quietly backed away wishing the adrenalin wasn't running down me leg and parked meself round the corner while I considered me options.

- Steam into him lashing out wildly and hope to spark him out before he had a chance to do me then hope Cosgrove really wasn't here.
- Sneak off and hope that I could find somewhere else to sleep before coming back early for me gear.
- Try talking me way out of the predicament I'd just found meself in
- Hope to fucking god that the twig that had just snapped behind me wasn't because it was under Cosgrove's foot

I spun round like a fucking loony tune to see three of them hoodie fuckers from earlier, that Duane one just kept staring at me the weird cunt, and I had an idea.

'That bloke round there owes me a hundred quid, if you can take it off him you can keep it.'

'What? Him at your front door Pagga or the one at the bottom of the stairs?'

Fuck, that's where Cosgrove was.

'The one at my door owes me money as well – where's the rest of your mob?'

'Round the corner – we come to straighten out what happened today.'

'I tell you what lads…and lass, we'll call it quits. You can have those blokes as a little peace offering – how's that?'

They fucking liked that and, after a little huddle, went in swinging. Cosgrove and Bobbin are handy fuckers but my charva army took them by surpise. They stood their ground for a minute but they were taking a lot of punishment and judging by the hands going in their pockets they was losing a lot of cash, there was claret everywhere and my two professional rivals decided to fuck off out of the way.

So job done, now I just needed to have a kip and sort some fresh gear out then in a few hours I'd be offski up the coast well out of the way of those two.

Told you I was a clever fucker.

CHAPTER 7

METRO-SEXUAL

'Progress Report 001.'
'Trojan in position sir.'
'Is he performing as expected?'
'Very much so sir.'
'Excellent. Keep me updated.'
'Yes Sir. Over and out.'

Next morning I was up and off. You know how blokes say they need a shit, a shower and a shave well I'm more of a wee, a wank and a weetabix man myself. All available cash was stashed in me socks, me special spy hearing gadget was in me pocket and the metro ticket they'd got me on expenses was safely grasped in my large, granite-like fist.

It was time. This sheriff was leaving town.

I had a quick peek through the blinds before leaving the flat. No sign of the two amigos but I waited until my taxi had pulled up before I opened the door – not through fear like, no way, just getting my head into spook mode see. Getting the old napper up to speed and in the game, sort of a warm up like for the dangerous world I was entering. I mean, you don't see footballers coming straight on the pitch without doing a bit of stretching do you? Actors and that have to pretend to be trees before they go on the stage don't they? Well it's the same with us officers of the King, we have to get the brain into gear before it's needed. So that's why I was careful about leaving the house. I wasn't scared like. Not of them two. Fuck off, I wasn't.

The station was mobbed. Some kind of exhibition going on up at the gay bit of town. Strange one really seeing all them blokes dressed as Dr. Spock and Captain Kirk holding hands and clutching little pink cases. There was some fucker dressed as Scotty as well running about with a big pink dildo shouting 'she canna take it captain, she canna take it.'

I didn't get it.

My new bird, who was never a bloke...ever, Vic, had said to wander round town a bit when I got up there like I was shopping. Then go and have a couple of pints and a bit of food somewhere before meeting her at the gate of the place when it got dark. She was dead specific an' all about not drawing attention to meself and not asking anyone questions about the place. Like I don't know that shit. Entry-level, basic spook stuff that is. Can't believe she thought I'd need a reminder about that, maybe it's cos' I'm new and she has to do it, like an induction for health and safety and that. Anyways, I put on me spook gear on the metro so I wouldn't stand out when I got there. Nowt flashy, just subtle so I blends in - I know the game matey don't you worry about that. It was difficult to try out me special newspaper with the hole cut out of it for spying purposes with me new shades on and the trilby I'd got kept falling off me head so I put the paper away and pretended to be asleep but really I had me spook listening device in masquerading as a music player thingy.

'Look at that cock with the big orange raincoat on.'

There's some right plebs on these trains like. They've fell for me disguise hook, line and sinker - probably think I'm some kind of actor or telly star.

'Is he touching himself through the pockets?'

Fuck me she's got good eyesight for her age.

'I think I recognise him from somewhere...Big Brother?'

Back of the net. It's official, this disguise is a winner.

'Nah. It's that Pagga fucker innit. Remember, he shagged you last week.'

'Oh, I'd blotted that shameful night out me mind. Here, pass the lambrini I cannot cope with the thought of that.'

If I remember right love you'd be better off drinking mouthwash.

Luckily it was my stop so I couldn't blow me disguise by giving them shit back but she was being blacklisted from the full Pagga experience in the future. I headed off round the town. The shops were bollocks and the cafe only done one sausage with the all-day breakfast so fuck that, I'm not wasting the King's money on rip-offs like that. Time for a pint and some crisps I reckon - don't want to be bloated with food later anyway if I'm going to be fighting to the death with a man with metal teeth or something do I?
I found a boozer and was pleasantly surprised to see the bar was proper comfy, almost like one of them Gentleman's Clubs in that London. And by 'Gentlemans Club' I don't mean the kind of place where Dirty Doreen from Denton throws things up her chuff while you eat pickled eggs.

Is that right? Or do I mean she throws pickled eggs up her chuff while you eat her? Anyways it wasn't that kind of Gents Club it was a bit posh, like Arthur Daley would have went to, even with a shit Minder like that Ray who replaced Terry - all hairdo and healthfoods that soft cockney twat. Anyways, looking round I felt right at home. This must be what happens when you works for the King. And, just so I knew I'd made it, just to bring home how I'd finally laid the ghost of my past, the barman was none other than Big Nose Brown. The spoiled-by-his-rich-parents, swotty, horrible fucker who'd spent every day of school life looking down on me.

'Can I help you sir?'

'Pint of lager and a packet of ready salted mate.'

'Certainly sir...that's not...?'

'Aye, Neville Palmer. Mr. Pagga to you Brown you twat.'

'Alright Nev...fucking hell, YOU'RE drinking in here? You need to pay with notes not copper you know.'

'Less of your cheek sunshine, you'll have the deep-sea divers in your hand as soon as I get me order. And just so you know they'll have been paid for by appointment to Her Majesty an' all so don't make me angry or you'll be slotted – and not in a good way either - know what I'm saying?'

'Right. Obviously I'm just kidding on. Lovely to see you again and that.'

'So you found your level in life then did you? As I remember you were going to follow daddy into the insurance business. Not work out then? Did they need someone with a bit of intelligence?'

'His firm went bust. Still this pays the bills. Anyway, lovely chatting with you but I need to get on. Enjoy your visit sir.'

'Yeah you run along. I'll call you if I want anything.'

Wanker – That's him told.

There's a load of suited types in the boozer and they're looking my way – they're impressed I can tell. They've heard the words 'Royal and 'Warrant' put two and two together, made four and now they can't hold my stare. Probably worried they'll get the old Brazilian treatment as if we was in London if they keep on looking and I don't mean on their pubes either. Aye, I think I'm gonna enjoy this life.

I settled back in me chair, confident that I'm the daddy in this place when I notice him. Skinny fucker, long mac, reading a big paper – one of them ones with no birds in with their tits out – and chewing a pen. Must be doing the crossword. What's made me notice him? I'll tell you. Every time I glance up the fucker's staring at me with hate in his eyes. Mebbe's I panelled him outside a bar or something one night? I don't recognise him like which is strange because I can remember most people I've hit. You know how some blokes can remember every bird they've ever shagged and some blokes can name all the cards in a pack and that? Well I can spot an ex-opponent a mile away and he wasn't one. Lucky for him like the weedy gimp.

But what was his fucking problem?

I resolved (see how I slip into spook mode) to find out and got up but, just as I was getting to him, I tripped on a wrinkle in the very expensive looking carpet and went flying into some old biddy sitting with her old fella.

'Oops sorry about that love – you'd think a place like this would be a big lump free zone wouldn't you?'

All polite and sophisticated even though I'm a bit embarrassed. This spook stuff comes natural to me.

'Why yes one would expect a place of this calibre to be free of big lumps – but that doesn't appear to be the case today.'

I disentangled meself taking care not to brush me hands on her chest – well it would be bad manners after I'd just took me face out of it – mind you she's got a cheek, I definitely felt a hand grab me cock when I was sprawled over her, dirty old mare. I just nod back at her and head to me seat taking a quick glance at the husband next to her – the old goats got a gleam in his eye and a hard on…eeeuurgh. I feel all dirty now.

'He's a big lad isn't he.'

Fucking upper classes – too much Rugby if you ask me.

By the time I'd been there a few hours I was starving, let's face it you don't get to my size without stocking up on the old carbs do you? I needed energy for all me training that I did – mind I hadn't been for a while – too busy pumping the lasses and looking after the one muscle that really mattered to have time to pump iron as well know what I mean. Anyway, I still needed to keep me strength up cos I'm a naturally athletic type anyway and my biceps don't need much work, in fact they more or less train theirselves. The last lass I had in the sack was right complimentary about us like, you know how the younguns use words like 'buff' and that these days to mean you're as good looking as fuck well she said I had 'moobs' and I while I didn't know what it meant I didn't let on, just another youngun word for handsome hunky fucker innit?

So I wandered to the pub kitchen pretending I was looking for the bogs. Some of the stuff in it was fucking old an all, I've shagged lasses younger than some of the pasties in that fridge, three quid an all...the robbing bastards. If I'd have had to pay for them I'd have been gutted, luckily there was no-one about - probably Pimm's O Clock or summit - so the vittles came my way for nowt. There's some people in the world might think that stealing four Cornish pasties and a pickled egg is a bit over the top but not me. My thinking was this, it was so easy that if I didn't nick them then some other fucker would and it would have preyed on me mind all the way there that some pikey fucker was eating food that should rightfully have been mine. Then I would have got to the job in a state of anxiety and the security of the nation would have been compromised (honestly I sound like a proper spook already don't I) you can't put a Cornish pasty ahead of the country's welfare now can you? Exactly, so shut up about it. I'm back in me seat necking the scran when I notice him again. Long Mac, skinny fucker staring us out. Now I hadn't forgotten about him, I am a professional spy now after all, but he'd slipped me mind for a second while I concentrated on topping up the old battery. This left us in a quandary, do I leave me last pasty on the table while I go over there and kick off with him, taking the risk that one of these buggers would nick it – that dirty old goat with the woman whose tits I'd just had me face in would probably shag it – or do I finish it first and take the chance that he might make a move while I'm otherwise engaged?

I took the third way, this is why my bird Victoria chose me because I can think outside the box – not strictly true like, most of me waking life is spent trying to get inside the box if I'm honest – keeping a close eye on skinny mac I rammed the entire pasty in me gob in one hit and got to me feet. It was need to know time. I stood over him while he pretended not to notice me, it probably looked like I was playing it cool but in reality I couldn't talk for pasty, actually I couldn't fucking breathe. So I was chewing away like a Police Alsation on a May Day protestors arse when he looked up.

'Fuck do you want fatty?'

I looked round to see who he was talking to – I hadn't realised there was a queue of us. Seeing no-one I twigged he was obviously mental. Seeing things and that. This changed my approach, I couldn't hit him now could I just cos he was two pigs short of a police station. I still couldn't talk, I tried so he could see I sympathised with his mentalness but all that came out was a grunt and a load of flaky bits of pastry and some gristle. After he'd wiped his face clean he tried to stand up but I pushed him back down, just to let him know that I understood his plight but obviously being mental he misunderstood this simple gesture and started shouting.

'FUCK DO YOU THINK YOU ARE YOU FAT FUCKER? YOU NICK ME BIRD OFF ME AND THEN START SHOVING ME ABOUT. WHY WOULD SHE FANCY A FAT FUCKER LIKE YOU I DON'T KNOW BUT YOU'RE THE REASON SHE'S DUMPED ME AND I'LL GET RID OF YOU IF IT'S THE LAST THING I DO YOU FAT PRICK.'

I looked round the pub and tried to re-assure people there was no problem.

'Eeees Mmuntal' I managed to get out between blasts of pasty flakes and dead dog. They seemed to understand and turned away, they didn't want to distract an officer of the King by making eye contact while I was busy did they?

So with that problem solved I turned to the other that was still sitting in his chair and shouting about me shagging his bird. He probably had a point, mini-me had been busy lately and she could have been one of dozens, I hoped it wasn't the one that had got handy with the dildo though, could be embarrassing if that got out. He looked like he was about to start shouting something like dildo so I acted quickly. Taking his mentalness into account and the fact that it wasn't really his fault he was acting like an arsehole and drawing attention to me I decided to use the velvet glove.

Still broke the fuckers nose first go like – you never lose it do you? - and there was some bad bastards in a warehouse round the corner about to find that out an all.

CHAPTER 8

SNEAKING IN THE BACK

'Progress Report 001.'
'Trojan en-route. Snatch team in position.'
'Good, good. Everyone briefed?'
'Of course sir. You can leave this to me. The plans will be back in the hands of the British Government tonight.'
'Excellent. Knew I could rely on you 001.'
'Thank You Sir. Over and out.'

Skinny Mac still hadn't come round by the time the sun was going down. Snotty swot Brown had been round a couple of times picking up glasses but I told him that the mental bastard had done a lot of ale and was sleeping it off. He wasn't overly happy with having a bloke spark out in his 'upmarket bar/grill' but couldn't really do much about it. He did want us to do something about the blood seeping from his nose though, so, just to keep the whinging get quiet, I stuffed me pasty wrapper up his nostrils. That's me being the nice one again eh? Say what you like about me but I don't hold a grudge, can't even hold a pint sometimes like, and it was in me nature to help the bloke out.

'No need to thank us Brown you swotty, snobby twat.'

'Where did you get that wrapper from Palmer, there's a load of pasties went missing from the kitchen earlier.'

'Well between you and me kidda I think sleeping beauty there had them away – look at the crumbs all over his face for a start eh? Anyway, I've got things to do so see you later you sad twat.'

And that was that. I got out the door and headed for the sinister looking building up the road. I'd obviously been in the boozer a while as it was pissing down and all dark and horrible looking outside. A copper car overtook me as I was halfway there and I got a good look at the bloke in the back – it was skinny Mac...and he was cuffed! I could see the copper next to him holding up a pasty wrapper accusingly and giving him the odd backhander. I was laughing at the fucker when he noticed us and started shouting and screaming and trying to point us out to the bizzy – proper mental like no doubt about it. Mind you the copper seemed to understand him – probably been on one of them courses they do instead of catching burglars- and he was turning my way.

Now I haven't got a warrant card or nowt and Vic told me that this mission was deniable - you won't know what that means but it's not good if you get caught...that's all I'm saying, so I had to think quick. The bizzy car screeched to a halt and the copper got out and walked towards me while his partner kept an eye on the mentalist. Gave him another slap an' all - good lad.

'Have you got a moment sir?'

I knew just how to play this.

'Of course Officer. How can I be of assistance?'

'It's a little absurd but we've arrested this man on suspicion of theft and vagrancy but he alleges that you assaulted him and were, in fact, the perpetrator of the crime for which he has been accused.'

'I think I recognise him. He was in the pub I had a mineral water in earlier, he was trying to sell me a pasty and when I explained I was allergic to them he began shouting at me so I left the pub.'

Brilliant.

'You're allergic to pasties?'

Cheeky fucker's looking at my belly.

'Yes Officer...and kebabs...'

Fuck it, in for a penny.

He's looking suspicious and lifting his radio to his mouth when his expression changes.

'You heading off up to the big Warehouse up the road sir?'

Shit.

'Yes. I've ehhmmm got an interview for a job.'

'At this time of night sir?'

'It's for a nightshift job.'

He's smiling now - I might have got away with this.

'Well good luck with that sir. My brother runs that place so I'll put in a word for you when I see him tomorrow.'

He's heading back to the car and I can hear him on his phone saying something about they've sent another one, big orange coat and a trilby, yeah...sunglasses in the dark, same place and I'll dispose of the evidence bruv. When I chance it.

'Cheers then Orifice.'

That's for the miners you twat.

He never flickers though, just keeps talking on the phone about there must be a manpower shortage if they're sending dildos like that now. He must be on about the police training centre given the state of some of them these days but I wonder what the other stuff was all about? Still no time for that, I've got undercover work to do for the King. When I get there it's all quiet round the front. Vic and the boys are obviously in there already like she said so rather than kick me heels and look suspicious I heads round the back to see if there's somewhere to get in and meet them out of sight.

Along the perimeter fence there's a hut and a gate and...bingo...the door's open. That'll do for me. As I'm heading towards the hut I see a light flash. Some dopey twat's sparked up a tab, I can see the end glowing - reminds me of a stag-do in Blackpool...no...no time for that - and it gets me blood boiling. Am I the only one who remembers the spook training? I runs up behind the bloke smoking the tab and cuffs him round the back of the head.

'Put that light out you doughnut!'

He hits the floor like a bag of shit. I don't knows me own strength me- I'm some kind of a lethal weapon like Mel Gibson before he turned mentalist...or is it racist? Can't remember. Anyways I done the bloke with one-punch and even if I did have a brick that I'd handily discovered just before I twatted him it's still classed as a one-blow knockout. So fuck off with your fair-fighting bollocks, the Marquis of Queensbury never came to my estate.

It's then I twig that the bloke what I've hit isn't actually a spook is he? No he's one of them, guarding the place isn't he. They should have known it would take more than one man to stop old Pagga - not fair on them really but I don't make the rules do I. I dragged him into the hut then surveyed me surroundings. The gate into the place at the back was now unguarded so I had a choice of holding the position (more spook talk eh? I'm a natural me!) for my new team to come this way or taking this bloke's gun and going in alone to capture all the glory and undoubtedly a gratitude hump off of Vic. There was no choice at all, with a mental picture of her naked, covered in baby oil and doing that pouty thing I grabbed mateys gun and swaggered on in there like John Wayne crossed with Clint Eastwood after they'd just done a twelve hour shift at a testosterone factory.

Pagga's coming you fuckers...and not in a good way neither.

CHAPTER 9

THE NAME'S PALMER…
PAGGA PALMER!

'*Progress Report. Confirm message receipt. Over.*'

'*Sir, Operation proceeding as planned. Over*'

'*And our late reserve? Is his performance acceptable? Over.*'

'*He's performing as expected Sir. Over.*'

'*Not what I asked. Is his performance commensurate with the trust placed in him by Her Majesty's Government? Over.*'

'*There's a strong possibility he may have been captured sir. Permission to extract? Over.*'

'*Denied. Burn him. Over.*'

'*Yes Sir. Over.*'

So I'm in and it's dead quiet. There's nee machinery blasting or owt. In fact there's no production of anything going on at all. I thought there might have been rockets being made to go to the moon or something or big fuck-off nuclear weapons aimed somewhere to kick off a massive war that would see arms dealers make shitloads of money but nah...nowt. The place is massive mind, reminds me of Dirty Stan's house when I was a kid. He was a case him though. Fucking tracksuit and gold chains all the time, used to get all the kids up at his and play hide and seek - thing was if he caught yer he played another game involving stuff being hidden. Eh? Well work it out you plum. For fuck's sake. Re-arrange these words then - Sausage, Hide, The. Give you a clue?

Right, anyways, now you've caught up I'll continue. Basically we was all raggy arsed little tearaways back then - you ended up raggy-arsed if he had his way an' all! - and he had pool tables, space-invaders, table tennis, records, colour telly and he always had pop and crisps on tap. You had to go in mob-handed though, safety in numbers and that. Do you ever watch them nature programmes on a Sunday night? Well you know how the wildebeest always get a drink or cross the river as a herd so they've got more chance of getting past the crocodiles, lions, fucking cheetahs and everyone else who wants a bit of their arse? It was the same at Dirty Stan's - he wanted a piece of your arse an' all only he didn't have teeth like a lion just a hard-on like an elephant and colostomy bag that stunk and gave him away if he sneaked in close while you was distracted by Moon Cresta.

I wanted to meet Charlie's Angels once and he said something like 'Stan'll fix it' and said to come into his office for a chat about it - never mind his office, what he meant was come in his mouth I reckon - I fucked off sharpish and never went back. Well I did, about ten years later in the middle of the night with a lorry - them pool tables never lose their value you know.

'Progress Report 001. Is target acquired?'

'Negative. Encountering Resistance. Clean up team will need to be prepared for major workload.'

'Assessment?'

'Target located. Resistance not enough to stop us. Operation will be completed.'

'And the decoy?'

'Lost eyes sir. No knowledge of location. Presumed deceased.'

'Sad but necessary. Keep me informed.'

'Yes Sir. Over and out.'

I've confused meself now. That's what happens see. You won't know this 'cos you're not as clever as me but I'll let you in on it. Your brain is like a big memory stick from a computer right? And you know you can only put so much porn...or other stuff...but mainly porn...on a stick before you run out of memory? Well your brain's just like that you can only fill it up so much before you runs out of space. Stands to reason don't it reallly. And as my brain's pretty full of porn then there ain't much room for owt else is there? And don't get all cocky and that either, by porn I mean shagging what I've done not something on a computer with a fucking droopy-tached bum bandit pretending he's into birds and that, poling some fit lass who wishes he was me and not a fucking hairy-lipped bender. Right? Good.

So I'm wandering round a big chamber that's got fuck all in it and trying to remember what the mission actually was. Did she tell us? All I can remember's her tits, the promise of five grand and maybe a good, hard shag. Come on Pagga, rack ya brain son...nah, just tits still. Fuck it - where's the bog in here, I've thought about her tits for too long now and these pants were tight to start with.

'Progress Report.'

'Resistance crushed. Gaining ground on target Sir.'

'Excellent. Keep focus and finish job.'

'Yes Sir. Over and out.'

Next thing I know is that while I've been thinking about Vic's jugs of joy a load of blokes with guns have got round us and I'm in the shit. Hold on...one of them's skinny mac bloke...and there's that copper...and snotty, swotty Brown. Fuck's going on here?

'Aah Mr Bond. I've been expecting you.'

Who's this fucking doylum then? Wearing some kind of sixties suit, baldy head, big scar through his eye and holding a cat.

Bender. Deffo.

'The name's Palmer...Pagga Palmer.'

Always wanted to say that mind. Could die a happy man now...well...if I was a hundred and five years old and I'd been nailing wor Vicky for the last sixty years anyway. Then I'd probably die happy.

'What?'

He looks confused. Proper pissed off even. Never mind that though - I gets to say it AGAIN!

'The name's Palmer...Pagg...'

'Alright Neville you big fat, stupid twat.'

For fucks sake! You have one ambition in life and then some wanker has to stamp all over it when you get near the bloody thing. Teachers was always saying 'Palmer, you'll be nothing - no ambition son.' While swot boy there was getting his hair ruffled and being told he'd go far - not fucking far enough if you ask me - and now, just cause I gets near the one thing in me life I did want to do he gets all jealous and blows it for me.

Hold on you sick-minded perv, I don't mean blows it like that do I? We ain't all like you is we?

And not content with stamping on my dream of saying 'The name's Palmer...Pagga Palmer...', raising me eyebrow and looking suave and sophisticated twice to a proper bona-fide super-villain in a high-tech super-villain type lair he says I'm fat an' all. Now I'm the kind of bloke who doesn't take criticism well. I'm aware that I haven't trained down the gym much lately - mainly because i've been busy - not because Cosgrove and Bobbin are always down there, no, that's not the reason. I've just been busy that's all. And for him to call me fat hurts my sensitive nature - yes I am sensitive, a man can be a fucking sex-god, able to drink his own weight in lager without falling over and be hard-as-fucking-nails and still be sensitive. And I am. I'm sensitive.

So I shot the cunt in the bollocks.

'I might be big, fat and stupid but I've still got a cock son.'

The rest lift up their weapons and all I can think of is that I never got to shag Vic. Gutted.

'I want him alive.'

Ha. The game's still on baby don't ditch them condoms yet.

And that was that really. Now we're back at the point where you found me. About to get me knackers flayed off with knotted rope because I can't actually tell them something I genuinely don't know. Still going to get kicked to death by Cosgrove and Bobbin if I get out of this and, most important of all, still in with a shout of nailing the lovely Vicky the spook. I know women me and remember, I am one clever fucker. If the first two are odds-on to happen then I reckon the last one is an' all. Might be tricky with flayed off knackers but I'll have a go.

Oh aye.

CHAPTER 10

GOT THE HUMP

'Progress Report.'

'Zero casualties sustained. Target in range. Expected mission accomplish three minutes.'

'Excellent. Your country owes you a great debt.'

'Just doing my job sir. Over and out.'

So, as I've said, I'm tied to a chair, stark-bollock naked, gonna get tortured, yadda yadda yadda. Think I'm bothered? Well you're wrong and I'm not even crying there's just loads of dust in here and I've got a bit of a sty in me eye that's all.

Anyways I'm not bothered. I once had a fight with Big Humper when I was a teenager and I wasn't scared of him neither.

Well...I was a bit.

Thing is though he was massive. Not muscley like what I am but fucking obese. Now you might think that's a easy fight but you'd be wrong. You're thinking 'Just dance round him, tire him out and then knock him out you dozy pillock,' ain't you? Well you're lucky I'm tied to this chair if you're thinking that you fucking gobshite.

You couldn't do that 'cos he was so fat his lard just swallowed up your punches unless you got in close enough to hit his chin but if you got close he bear-hugged you till you couldn't breathe and when you came round you found out why he was called Big Humper. If you hadn't worked it out then the blood running down your leg and the pain in your arse gave you the idea. That was his thing see - if he beat you then you got shagged and it put you off fighting him in the first place. It was all mind games so nobody chanced their arse virginity and thus he rose up the fighting ladder on the estate unchallenged.

Then one day he knocked my kebab out me hand...

Don't know if I've mentioned this but we was poor growing up. So poor we didn't have satellite telly or nothing. They talk about kids in poverty these days but sometimes it was all I could do to nick fifty quid out of the old dear's purse. They don't know they're born these days they really don't.

Anyways, he knocked me kebab to the floor and stood there laughing with his little squad of hangers-on and bum-boys. My crew looked up to me as the leader even then so I had to do something.

'I'm gonna fucking batter you for that Humper.'

He just smiled, grabbed his cock and looked at mine. Fucking shiver went up my spine and I mentally started saying goodbye to my arse cherry.

'I'll do you tomorrow Palmer...and I do mean DO YOU.'

He turned to walk off but I realised then and there what was happening. He was putting the fear into me so's when tomorrow came I'd either shit it and not turn up thus giving him another notch on his fighting scorecard or I'd be so paralysed with fear 'cos I'd thought about it all night that I'd be soft as shite and get a good fucking...in more ways than one. There was only one thing to do. As he turned, I picked up a brick from where we kicked the shop's new wall in to raid the sweets, and twatted him over the head from behind. He went down like a sack of shite and his so-called mates were on him in seconds. From big Humper to Big Rumper in one quick move.

And that's what these fuckers are doing with the whole bollock naked, tied to a chair shit. If they're gonna slot me then they're gonna slot me. And if it's gonna hurt then it's gonna hurt. I can't do nothing about it so I ain't gonna worry, then if the chance comes that I can do something about it I'll be ready and not paralysed with fear.

Told you I was a clever fucker.

CHAPTER 11

THE CLIMAX

'Progress Report.'

'Target neutralised. Mission accomplished Sir.'

'Good, good. Return to base.'

'Sir. Demise of decoy not yet confirmed. Permission to check?'

'Denied. Mission accomplished. Back to base.'

'Sir. Say again. You're breaking up. Repeat, demise of decoy not yet confirmed. Permission to check?''

'Denied. Repeat DENIED.'

'Breaking up sir. Cannot understand. Permission assumed. Over and out.'

There's loads of shouting and shooting outside - bit like that stag do I went on in Blackpool when Head-the-ball Henry woke up in that tranny bar actually - and the two guards are a bit nervous looking. Eventually they have a bit of a conflab and decide who's going out to have a look.

Well, I say a conflab, it's a fucking big argument really. One of them ones where they try to keep their voices down and look normal for the public, ie me, but really neither of them's backing down 'cos they're both too scared to go out there. Luckily me spy hearing thing's still stuck in me lug so I can hear every word that's said.

'Go and check then.'

'Fuck off. Who put you in charge?'

'I'm the number five henchman, you're number ten or something so get out there.'

'Number five...number ten? What fucking books do you read you plum? There's loads of friggin' bullets flying out there dickhead!'

At this point I had a very bad feeling that bullets were going to start flying in here and the shitness of these two would make sure I got one of the fuckers so I tried to lighten the atmosphere a bit.

'I'll go out and have a look...'

'Gag that prick.'

Bollocks.

At this point a top spy would have a plan and somehow disarm the bloke stupid enough to get close in to him while trying to gag him. He would chin him, take his gun, shoot the other one by using the first's body as a shield and then make his escape, probably nailing a couple of top models on the way out.

Sadly I'm only a trainee so I got what looked...and tasted...like a distinctly sweaty pair of underpants stuffed in me gob. Don't ask how I know what sweaty underpants taste like either, not now we're starting to get on eh? Round about now as well, a top spy would have his secret gadget what he'd been given in the lead up to the mission and he would find a way of using it to escape, do the disarming, killing and nailing the top models thing before killing the baddie and saving the world.

And I still had me ear thing!

I worked out that if I twisted me head left and down, then pretended to sneeze whilst jerking (stop sniggering - we're not at school now are we?) me head rapid like then it would fall into me left palm. I could then use the sharp edge on it - from where i'd tried to make sparks on the wall behind the 'Badger' when I was going to set fire to Billy the Liar - to cut open the ropes what were holding us before pretending I wanted to tell them something dead important and knocking fuck out of the one that got closest when I kidded on I couldn't talk loud. Then I could use him as a human shield, kill the second one with his gun, finish the mission...whatever the fuck it was...and sort Vicky out bigstyle. Fucking mint, let's do it.

'What's that thing that's just fell out of his ear and passed his outstretched hand onto the floor?'

Bollocks.

'Looks like a kids toy.'

Fucking amateurs.

Then one of them gets a burst of static and some garbled shite on his walkie-talkie. I can't quite make out what's said though.

'Fat lump was a decoy. Real team are here and are taking Mr. Vest and the secret plans. Kill him and get up here.'

Nah. Must have been in French or something.

'I said kill him and get up here.'

I haven't a clue what they're talking about me mind. The reception's terrible on that thing. The two doughnuts in here are heading over with their guns out though - probably to surrender and beg for mercy. Aye...that'll be it.

'Stop pissing about. We NEED YOU NOW. KILL HIM!'

You'd think they'd have invested in better kit really. Fucking second-division super-villain if you ask me. Like that pretend football team in Milton Keynes that all real fans hate, this fucker's just playing at it with his shit lair and his walkie-talkies what don't even work so the henchmen don't even know what they're supposed to do and think they have to kill people who are top doormen and protection officers and the dust in here's unbelievable, fucking super-villain my arse, I've got loads of water in me eye 'cos of this dust.

And as some long-haired American fop once said, I'm staring down a bullet when one part of me decides to make his final stand...good lad.

I manage to spit the sweaty kegs out of me gob so I can go out with a bit of dignity at least.

'He's telling you to fuck off an' all you pair of clowns,' the dust in here's fucking terrible mind, cannot see for water now, 'My name's Pagga Palmer and I grew up with nowt but I made something of meself so you pricks do what you have to do 'cos I've had a good life and this'll be a good death!'

Oh, I hope there's cctv in here 'cos that'll look fucking brilliant on the news when they find me body!

Then I shut me eyes and wait for the end.

*

Two loud bangs and me first thought is *'Ha! that didn't hurt at all.'* So I opens me peepers and there's two dead henchmen what've stopped arguing for ever. Mint. Even better though, wor Vic was stood in front of us all sweaty and slippery and it fair got me blood up again I can tell you.

'Oh...I was hoping you'd be in proportion Mr. Palmer.'

Bitch.

God I love her.

'Off you go chaps. I'll take care of relieving Mr. Palmer here.'

Then, as soon as they're out and it's just me and her, she slips off her gear and stands there to give us a look for a brief second in the light by the exploding factory before climbing on.

I knew she fancied us. Told you I was clever.

'Mr. Palmer...Pagga...there's something I have to tell you.'

'I fucking knew you was a bloke!'

There's a proper wicked smile on her face.

'I think I like you tied up my little Geordie friend.'

'Little? Fuck off love. Oooh that's nice.'

'Anyway my name isn't actually Victoria, it's Emily.'

Oh right. Spook names and that, I get it. So I get to call you Emily from now on when we're doing secret mission and that pet then?'

'Well, my friends call me Em...'

Epilogue

One Year Earlier

Victorias Secret

He was about thirty, shaven headed and loud. His companions were similar and they appeared to enjoy the effect they had. Relished the fear in ordinary faces and revelled in the feeling of power as Joe public shrank back from them. Profanity preceding them like a rabbit round a dog track as they made their way down the street.

She'd positioned the red dot on the ring leader's head for three seconds without pulling the trigger, the shouting in her earpiece telling her to get on with it, before deciding it would be much more fun to let these boys feel some of the pain they so enjoyed giving out.

Pocketing her gun she'd stepped into the street, saying softly 'Want some action boys?'

Shaking her head at the memory, she manipulated the cocktail shaker violently, she hated making Mojito's, particularly the inference from whomever had requested it that she wasn't quite as good at them as they were used to.

I bloody went to public school, learnt things like tap and modern dance. I can hold conversations for hours about politics and world affairs and now I'm working in a bloody bar , she thought bitterly. And not just any bar, Victoria had ended up in 'Vault' aptly named as a haunt of bankers, businessmen, gangsters and playboys. She knew she wouldn't be here long but still disliked the place enough to hate her every waking minute here.

Still it's my own fault, she thought, handing over the drink to the ponytailed eighties throwback that was now leering at her, should have listened to daddy but no, I had to make my own way in the world didn't I.

Ponytail was making improper suggestions. She knew she looked good, ice blue eyes under blonde hair, the worlds prettiest smile – well so she'd been told - a cut glass accent that turned men to jelly apparently and a very inviting cleavage. He didn't seem to realise that the invitation wasn't actually extended to him and did his best to introduce himself to her chest region, pausing his descent into her blouse only when a suited arm grabbed him roughly round the neck and unceremoniously hauled him away.

The Geordie bouncer definitely had a thing for her and, if truth be told, she'd easily reciprocate if the chance arose but sadly, the cleavage wasn't for him either, not tonight at least. She glanced round the room and caught the eye of the man she'd set out to snare. He appeared to have some difficulty focusing as first her right breast and then her left got his undivided attention before he managed to look her in the eye.

Victoria, knowing that her new, sexy, bought for the occasion, lacy brassiere was showing her off to her fullest extent gave him a naughty smile before turning away to cover herself up, her mind taking her back to just why she'd ended up in this place.

Shaven head had come forward, leering at the blonde girl who was obviously game for a bit. He'd put out his hand to grab her, looking back at his steroid-addled friends to ensure he had an audience.

Victoria had snapped his wrist with one movement and buried a booted foot deep in his groin with another, his howls of pain had been silenced only by the sound of two black vans screeching up alongside the group and bundling them all in.

Her commanding officer at Thames house had been less than pleased with her performance and she'd been sent on this mission to find out about the latest target and his apparently wealth despite not having any means of accumulating it. He was beside her now, patting her arse and she sighed inwardly. When she was recruited she had said she'd do these things in the interest of national security but had rather hoped it would be with fit young oil barons and fellow spies not middle aged, perma tanned, petrol heads. Still, she thought, glancing over at the Geordie bouncer as he stood impassively at the end of the bar, I'll make sure there'll be another time for some fun with him when this is over.

Printed in Great Britain
by Amazon